SPOTLIGHT ON NATIVE AMERICANS

DELAWARE
(LENAPE)

Joseph Stanley

press.

New York

Published in 2016 by The Rosen Publishing Group, Inc.
29 East 21st Street, New York, NY 10010

First Edition

Editor: Katie Kawa
Book Design: Samantha DeMartin
Material reviewed by: Donald A. Grinde, Jr., Professor of Transnational/American Studies at the State University of New York at Buffalo.

Library of Congress Cataloging-in-Publication Data

Names: Stanley, Joseph, author.
Title: Delaware (Lenape) / Joseph Stanley.
Description: New York : PowerKids Press, [2016] | Series: Spotlight on Native
  Americans | Includes index.
Identifiers: LCCN 2015038753 | ISBN 9781508141150 (pbk.) | ISBN 9781508141167 (6 pack) |
ISBN 9781508141181 (library bound)
Subjects: LCSH: Delaware Indians–Juvenile literature.
Classification: LCC E99.D2 S89 2016 | DDC 974.004/97345–dc23
LC record available at http://lccn.loc.gov/2015038753

Manufactured in the United States of America

CPSIA Compliance Information: Batch #BW16PK: For Further Information contact Rosen Publishing, New York, New York at 1-800-237-9932

CONTENTS

FAR FROM HOME

CHAPTER 1

The Delaware people got their name from the Delaware River, which flows through the homelands their **ancestors** settled in long before Europeans arrived in North America. The name "Delaware" was given to them by British colonists. The Delaware people are also known by their traditional name—Lenape or Lenni Lenape. In their native language, those names mean "people" or "original people."

The Lenape people have faced many struggles throughout their history. Their population was cut down by disease and war. They were later forced off their homelands and made to move west. However, the Lenape people are still trying to keep their **culture** alive, even though the different groups of Lenape **descendants** live far apart from each other.

There are over 16,000 Lenape descendants currently living in North America. Some live as part of federally recognized groups in Oklahoma and Wisconsin. Others live closer to their ancestral homelands in New Jersey, Pennsylvania, and Delaware. Some Lenapes also live in Canada. No matter where these people live, though, they're connected by a shared history and culture.

The Delaware River was very important to the Lenape people. Some still live close to this river, while others live far away in the lands the U.S. government forced them to move to in the 1800s.

LIVING ON LENAPE LANDS

CHAPTER 2

The Lenape homelands were in the eastern part of what's now the United States. Their homelands extended from present-day Cape Henlopen, Delaware, to Long Island in what's now New York State. This included parts of present-day Pennsylvania and New Jersey, too.

The early Lenape people were deeply connected to the natural world around them. They traveled on the many waterways surrounding them in wooden canoes they made by hand. They also fished in these waters and hunted animals in the forests around them. Farming played a large part in Lenape life, too. While the men hunted, the women farmed the land. They grew crops such as corn, beans, and squash. Lenape women also

Lenape wigwam

gathered wild plants to eat, including berries. The Lenape people came together to form large farming communities in the summer.

The Lenape people often lived in round houses called wigwams. However, they sometimes built larger longhouses to hold more than one family. These homes were made using materials found in nature, such as animal skins and tree bark.

Wigwams were smaller and easier to move, so the Lenape people used them while they hunted in the summer. Longhouses stayed in one place and were often winter homes.

Lenape longhouse

DIFFERENT GROUPS

CHAPTER 4

The Lenape people were divided into three smaller groups. These groups were separated by where they lived and the **dialect** of the Lenape language they spoke. The Munsee people generally lived in the northern parts of the Lenape homelands. The Unami people lived in the central areas of Lenape land. The Unalachtigo people lived south of the Unami.

Within these groups, there were also three main clans, which were based on the mother's **heritage**. This meant that if a mother belonged to one clan, then her children would belong to that same clan. These clans were known as the Turkey clan, the Wolf clan, and the Turtle clan. However, some historians believe the Munsee people didn't have a Turtle clan. This clan system held the three groups of Lenape people together, despite their differences in language and location.

A governing council for each group of Lenape people was made up of leaders from each of these clans. They were known as *sachems,* or chiefs.

The Lenape people lived in a matrilineal society, which meant descent was traced through the mother's line.

WAR AND DISEASE
CHAPTER 5

When Europeans began arriving in North America, they traded with Native Americans for furs, which the Europeans then sold in their home countries. The Dutch were common trading partners with the Lenape in the early days of European colonization.

However, other groups of Native Americans wanted to be able to trade with the Dutch. One of these groups was the Susquehannock people. In the 1630s, the Susquehannock people waged war against the Lenape. At the same time, diseases began to take their toll on the Lenape. With their population reduced, the Lenape people were defeated by the Susquehannock, who then controlled the Lenape.

Susquehannock man

By the late 1600s, the Lenape population had decreased sharply because of war and disease. Because diseases such as **smallpox** were brought to North America by Europeans, the Lenape had never been exposed to them before. Unlike the Europeans, the Lenape hadn't built up **immunity** to these diseases, so they died in large numbers. Other Native American groups also suffered the same fate.

This historical illustration shows the Lenape people interacting with Europeans in what would become the colony of Pennsylvania.

THE WALKING PURCHASE
CHAPTER 6

In 1682, British settlers led by William Penn landed in what would become the colony of Pennsylvania. Penn and the Lenape leaders had a friendly relationship. A peace **treaty** was signed between them, and Penn respected the Lenape people. He purchased land from them instead of immediately claiming that it belonged to England.

However, Penn's son Thomas didn't respect the Lenape the way his father did. He was the driving force behind the Walking Purchase of 1737. After William Penn's death, colonial leaders in Pennsylvania claimed to have found a treaty from 1686 stating that the Lenape would give the colonists as much land as a person could walk in 1.5 days. Thomas Penn found the three fastest men in Pennsylvania and promised a prize to the man who ran the farthest in this amount of time.

The fastest man covered over twice the land the Lenape had expected. This caused the Lenape people to lose much of their land. They were forced to relocate to areas such as Ohio.

The Lenape and the colonists in Pennsylvania traded with each other and had a good working relationship. That good relationship changed, however, with the Walking Purchase.

15

TIMES OF WAR
CHAPTER 7

The Walking Purchase had a lasting effect on the relationship between the British and the Lenape. During the French and Indian War, which lasted from 1754 to 1763, most members of the Lenape people sided with the French at first and fought against the British. However, there were some Lenape leaders who supported the British.

During the war, the Lenape signed another treaty that forced them to move even farther west into what's now western Pennsylvania and Ohio. The Treaty of Easton was signed in 1758, and it was the next step in the removal of the Lenape from their homelands.

The Lenape were also divided during the American Revolution, which lasted from 1775 to 1783. Some supported the British, but others supported the American colonists. In 1778, the Lenape became the first Native American group to sign a peace treaty with the United States government, which was then known as the Continental Congress. This treaty was signed at Fort Pitt, which is now Pittsburgh, Pennsylvania.

The French and Indian War was fought between the French and their Native American allies and the British and their Native American allies. Some groups of Lenape people allied with the British, and some with the French.

MOVING WEST
CHAPTER 8

In the late 1700s, the Lenape joined with other groups of Native Americans living on the frontier to fight against the U.S. government. They didn't want the government to take any more of their lands. However, these Native Americans were defeated at the Battle of Fallen Timbers in 1795. After this defeat, they signed the Treaty of Greenville, which stated that they would never fight against the U.S. government again.

After signing the Treaty of Greenville, the Lenape were forced out of what would become Ohio. This led to the dispersal, or scattering, of the Lenape people. Some moved to present-day Indiana and then to

Shown here is a Lenape home on a **reservation** in Kansas in the 1800s.

present-day Kansas. By 1867, this group of Lenape people was relocated to what's now Oklahoma. Another group of Lenape people **migrated** to Canada, while others were sent to live on a reservation in what's now Wisconsin.

Reservation life in Oklahoma and Wisconsin wasn't easy for the Lenape people in the nineteenth and early twentieth centuries. They often lived in poverty, and they were expected to give up their traditional way of life.

This painting shows the signing of the Treaty of Greenville.

FEDERAL RECOGNITION

CHAPTER 9

Currently, there are three federally recognized Lenape communities in the United States. This means these groups are now able to govern themselves with the support of the U.S. government.

The Delaware Nation has its headquarters in Anadarko, Oklahoma. The Delaware Tribe of Indians is another federally recognized Lenape community, centered in Bartlesville, Oklahoma. It also has a branch with headquarters in Caney, Kansas. Members of the Stockbridge-Munsee Community live around Bowler, Wisconsin.

Each of these federally recognized groups has special programs and departments designed to keep Lenape culture alive. For example, the Delaware Nation has a Cultural Preservation Department that runs programs such as language classes. In these classes, members of the Delaware Nation learn the Lenape language spoken by their ancestors.

These groups also have different forms of government. The Delaware Nation has a president and vice president. The Stockbridge-Munsee Community and the Delaware Tribe of

Indians are both governed by councils, which are led by chiefs. These governing groups make decisions for the community and help set up social services within the community.

The Lenape Center, which is located on the island of Manhattan in New York, was created to preserve and promote Lenape art, culture, and language. Two of its founders, Joe Baker and Curtis Zunigha, are members of the Delaware Tribe of Indians. The third founder, Hadrien Coumans, is an adopted member of the White Turkey/Fugate family of Lenape descent.

Curtis Zunigha

Hadrien Coumans

WORKING TOWARD A BETTER LIFE

CHAPTER 10

Each of the federally recognized groups of Lenape people runs businesses. The Delaware Tribe of Indians runs a gift shop in Bartlesville. The Delaware Nation also runs a gift shop, as well as a solar energy development project. The Stockbridge-Munsee Community runs businesses that include a **casino** and hotel, a convenience store, and a gas station.

These communities also have special departments created to provide social services for the Lenape people. Care for children and the elderly is especially important in these communities. They also offer assistance to people looking for housing. Poverty is still a concern in these communities, and many Lenape people need help looking for low-cost housing.

The Delaware Tribe of Indians and the Stockbridge-Munsee Community also have wellness centers designed to help the members of their community stay healthy. Good health care wasn't always available to the Lenape living on reservations. These wellness centers aim to provide the best possible health care to the people who visit them.

Life has changed a lot for the Lenape people since they first came to Kansas, Oklahoma, and Wisconsin. They have more opportunities now, but their leaders still want to create businesses and social programs to improve their quality of life even more.

EASTERN LENAPE COMMUNITIES

CHAPTER 11

While many Lenape people live in Oklahoma, Kansas, or Wisconsin, others live closer to their original homelands. These Lenape people are working hard to restore their traditional culture in places where it once seemed lost forever.

The Lenape Nation of Pennsylvania is a group of Lenape people who work to educate the public about Lenape history and culture. They run a trading post and gift shop selling traditional Lenape arts and crafts. They also run a cultural center in Easton, Pennsylvania.

Another Lenape community has its headquarters in Bridgeton, New Jersey. The Nanticoke Lenni-Lenape Tribal Nation was formed out of clans and churches that governed themselves through the 20th century. By the 1970s, this community was led by a council, and today it has a constitutional government.

The Nanticoke Lenni-Lenape Tribal Nation runs a tribal store, which also displays historical **artifacts** from the

Lenape people, as well as other Native American groups. In addition, this nation runs a **powwow** every year that's open to the public. Spring and fall gatherings are also held just for members of this community.

The Nanticoke Lenni-Lenape people show their traditional arts and crafts at festivals meant to introduce the public to their culture.

PRESERVING LENAPE CULTURE

CHAPTER 12

Cultural preservation is important to every Lenape community in the United States and Canada. Each community has come up with its own ways to keep Lenape culture alive. The Internet has become a useful tool for sharing Lenape culture and history with the rest of the world.

The Nanticoke Lenni-Lenape Tribal Nation has partnered with the Nanticoke Indian Tribe of Delaware and the Lenape Indian Tribe of Delaware to create an online museum and learning center. This online resource features information on Lenape history, videos of Lenape powwows, and articles about Lenape games, spiritual beliefs, and even medicine.

The Delaware Tribe of Indians is also working in a creative way to protect and preserve Lenape culture. One special area of focus for this community is the Lenape language. In 2002, the Lenape Language Preservation Project started the process of creating the Lenape Talking Dictionary. This website features over 15,000 words in the Lenape language, and it's still growing. It also features traditional Lenape stories and songs in their native language. The Lenape Talking Dictionary was made possible through grants from the National Science Foundation.

Shown here is Lenape Park in Pennsylvania, which got its name from the Native American community that called Pennsylvania home long before it was given that name by Europeans.

MANY PLACES, ONE IDENTITY

CHAPTER 13

Survival hasn't been easy for the Lenape people. They were once known as the "grandfathers" of a huge community of Native Americans. However, wars and diseases caused their numbers to shrink and their power to decline. Many of them were sent far from their homelands to live on reservations, where they struggled to preserve their traditional way of life.

Despite all the challenges the Lenape faced, they held on to their identity and worked hard to share that identity with the world. Elders passed down stories, such as their creation story, and taught younger generations about the history of their people. These elders also became the last surviving link to the Lenape language, which modern Lenape leaders are working to preserve and protect.

Lenape descendants live throughout North America—from Canada to Oklahoma. Although they live in different places, they're united by a shared past and a shared culture. Whether they're called Delaware, Lenape, or Lenni Lenape, they're all descendants of the "original people."

The Lenape people have worked hard to preserve their culture for the next generation. They take great pride in their traditional way of life.

GLOSSARY

ancestor: Someone in your family who lived long before you.

artifact: Something made by humans in the past.

casino: A building used for gambling.

culture: The beliefs and ways of life of a certain group of people.

descendant: Someone related to a person or group of people who lived at an earlier time.

dialect: A form of language spoken in a certain area that uses some of its own words, grammar, and pronunciations.

heritage: The traditions and beliefs that are part of the history of a group or nation.

immunity: Bodily power to resist a disease.

migrate: To move from one place to another.

powwow: A Native American social gathering.

reservation: Land set aside by the government for a specific Native American group or groups to live on.

smallpox: A serious disease that causes a fever and a rash and is often deadly.

status: Position or rank in relation to others.

treaty: An official agreement made between two or more countries or groups.

FOR MORE INFORMATION

BOOKS

Bial, Raymond. *The Delaware*. New York, NY: Marshall Cavendish Benchmark, 2005.

Hìtakonanulaxk. *The Grandfathers Speak: Native American Folk Tales of the Lenapé People*. New York, NY: Interlink Books, 2005.

Levine, Michelle. *The Delaware*. Minneapolis, MN: Lerner Publications Company, 2007.

WEBSITES

Due to the changing nature of Internet links, PowerKids Press has developed an online list of websites related to the subject of this book. This site is updated regularly. Please use this link to access the list: www.powerkidslinks.com/sona/del

INDEX